possible initial cons⸏⸏⸏⸏⸏⸏⸏⸏⸏⸏⸏⸏⸏⸏⸏⸏⸏⸏⸏e
double initial consc⸏⸏⸏⸏⸏⸏⸏⸏⸏⸏⸏⸏⸏⸏⸏⸏⸏⸏e
of these can be 'bui⸏⸏⸏⸏⸏⸏⸏⸏⸏⸏⸏⸏⸏⸏⸏o
letters, but it is far bե⸏⸏⸏⸏⸏⸏⸏⸏⸏⸏ to learn them
as one combined sound. Often, sounds such as
'sh' in *ship* and 'ch' in *chop,* cannot be built
anyway. The initial consonants plus vowel often
represent the first vital syllable in any word.

The books show one main word, with its full-
colour illustration, together with clues to additional
words, in line only, at the foot of the page. Extra
words using the same sounds are given for refer-
ence and conversation. Parents and teachers
should emphasise the combined effect of consonant and vowel, making possible the reading of
the whole first syllable. This will prove a great aid
to children tackling new words in later reading.
If the illustration does not provide sufficient clue,
the full starting sound of consonant plus vowel
should be given.

Recognising individual letters is essential if the
full value of phonic training is to be obtained, so
it is important for children to *write* the letters at
the same time as learning to say them. Writing
practice reinforces memory, a vital part of a child's
learning process.

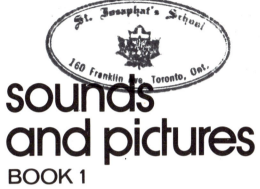

sounds
and pictures
BOOK 1

by MERVYN BENFORD
illustrated by GERALD WITCOMB

Ladybird Books Loughborough

a

apple

more words to say
acrobat, ash, add, atom, atlas

You might find both of these
in the woods.

ba

bag

more words to say
bandit, bank, bad, barrow, bang

What are these ?

ca

camera

more words to say
cap, cannon, catch, cabin, can, cash,
carol, camp

Do you know these creatures?

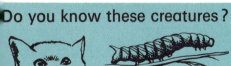

da

dagger

more words to say
dash, dazzle, daddy, dab, damp

What are these called?

fa

fan

more words to say
fancy, fantastic, fat, fashion

Perhaps the father of this works in this.

ga

garage

more words to say

gas, gap, gag, gallon, gather,
gang, gadget

Horses like to do this.

ha

hammer

more words to say
ham, have, has, happen, happy,
handkerchief, habit

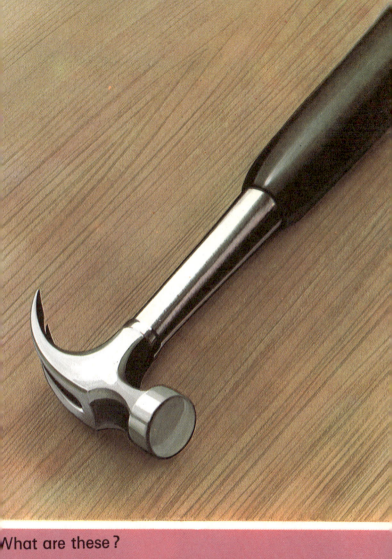

What are these?

ja

jam

more words to say

jacket, javelin, jazz, January, jam

The garage uses it to lift up a car.

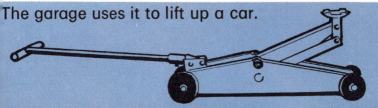

la

lamb

more words to say
latch, language, lap, land

What is this . . .   and this ?

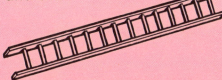

ma

magnet

more words to say
map, magic, mad, man, manners

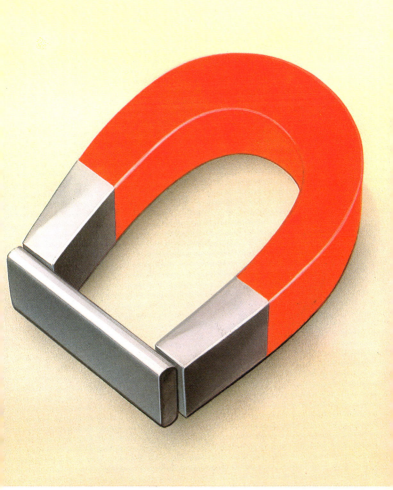

Please wipe your feet on this . . .

but don't play with these.

pa

parachute

more words to say
parrot, pattern, passage, panel, palace

What are these ?

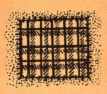

ra

rabbit

more words to say
rags, ran, rap, rang, rapid, ramble

A baby plays with this . . .

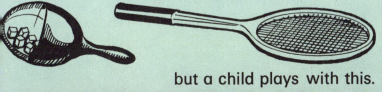

but a child plays with this.

sa

saddle

more words to say

salad, sand, sad, sack, savage,
satisfy, satellite

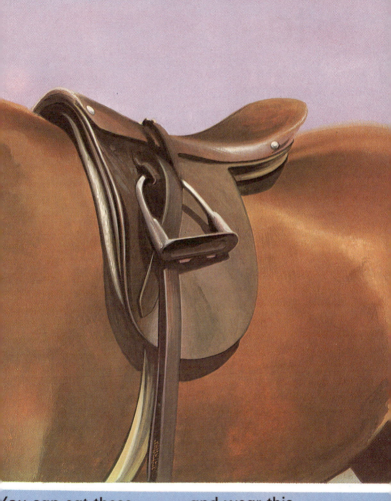

You can eat these . . .   and wear this.

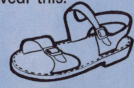

ta

tank

more words to say
tap, tackle, tacks, tax, tangle, tablet, tan

What are these?

a

apron

more words to say
ace, ape, age, ache, alien

You find this on a Christmas tree

and this on an oak tree.

ba

bacon

more words to say
basin, bale, bathe, baker, base

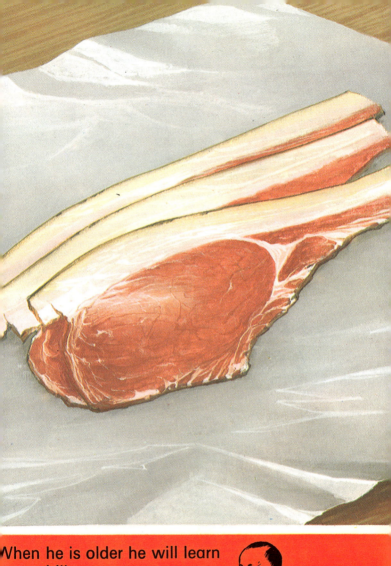

When he is older he will learn to read like you.

ca

cage

more words to say
cable, cake, came, cave

da

dates

more words to say
danger, day, dale, dame

fa

face

more words to say
favourite, fade, famous, fate

ga

gate

more words to say
game, gale, gave, gape

la

lake

more words to say
lane, lady, lazy, late, labour

Can you tie these . . .  and this ?

ma

mane

more words to say
make, male, mate, major, made

na

name

more words to say
navy, native, nation, nature

NAOMI WITCOMB

BROWNIEWEAR
by UMBRO ㉗

12% TERYLENE 33% COTT

pa

pastry

more words to say
paper, paste, pace, pale, patient

This book has these.

ra

radio

more words to say
race, radar, rate, range

What are these?

sa

safe

more words to say
sale, save, sake

2 These two numbers
are the - - - - **2**

ta

table

more words to say
taste, take, tame, tale

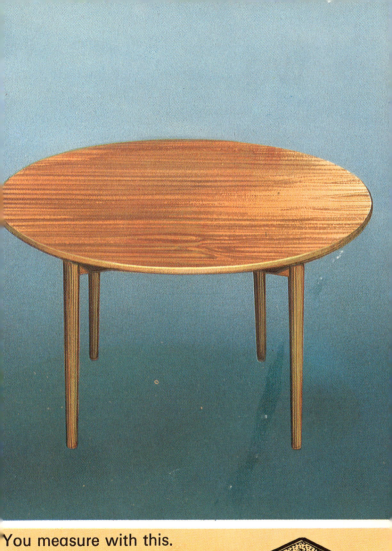

You measure with this.

wa

waves

more words to say
wafer, wages, wake, wade